Los Angeles Collegiate Playwrights Festival Vol. 1

Los Angeles Collegiate Playwrights Festival Vol. 1

Edited by James Elden

A Punk Monkey Productions Publication

Los Angeles Collegiate Playwrights Festival Vol. 1

Punk Monkey Productions
North Hollywood, CA

First Punk Monkey Productions Printing, 2019

For Colleen

CONTENTS

PREFACE

The Los Angeles Collegiate Playwrights Festival premiered in the spring of 2018 with the intention of bringing the work of aspiring college playwrights to the stage with the assistance of industry professionals active in the Hollywood community. Within these pages are the six plays selected to represent the inaugural season of LACPF. Each piece offers a unique perspective to the everyday struggles of love, loss, and the ongoing pursuit and discovery of one's identity within themselves and their external environment. The purpose of this publication is not only to share these stories and inspire other up-and-coming playwrights to cultivate their creativity but also to provide material for amateur and professional performers and directors alike with fresh material and insight into the everyday challenges we all face. It is through the art of storytelling and performance that we are able to find common ground, understanding, and a means of escape in this ever-changing world. I hope you enjoy reading these plays as much as we enjoyed the honor of breathing them to life. I hope perhaps that you may be inspired to bring these stories and the subsequent volumes that follow to the stage and share them with your community. Enjoy, and break a leg in all your creative pursuits.

- James Elden

Zap

By Sean Dunnington

Sean Dunnington

Sean Dunnington, from the Big Island of Hawai'i, is pursuing his degree in "Playwriting, Creative Process, and Literary Analysis" at the Johnston Center for Integrative Studies at the University of Redlands, class of '19. He recently returned from the London Academy of Music and Dramatic Arts with a diploma in the Classical Acting Programme. Currently, he is residing in New York City, working as a literary intern at the Vineyard Theatre. Sean's recent playwriting credits include *Flat Fish* (NYC Fresh Grind Festival), *Zap* (Los Angeles Collegiate Playwrights Festival), *Bonkers for Bonkers* (NYC Gay Pride Plays), and *The Undocumented* (NYC Sugartown Shorts & Manhattan Repertory Theatre). He is a member of The Dramatists Guild of America. Visit him at www.seandunnington.com.

Zap was originally produced by Punk Monkey Productions at The Lounge Theatre in Hollywood, CA in May 2018. It was directed by Shaun Landry. The lighting design was by Michael Massey. The board operator and stage manager was Jany Stehman. The cast was as follows:

Jessica White.....................................Jessica Park
Mom..Jessica Abrams
Dad...Rich Cassone
Director...Mark Motyl
Boyfriend...Eli Magers
Gale....................................Melibelle Lavandier
Danielle......................................Lisa Goodman

CHARACTERS:

(IN ORDER OF APPEARANCE)
JESSIE, a young woman, conflicted yet persistent, searching, early twenties.
MOM, Jessie's mother, purposeful, initiator, late forties.
DAD, Jessie's father, nostalgic, follower, late forties
DIRECTOR, a man of control and authority, knows what he wants, older.
GALE, Jessie's female lover, unapologetically queer, just answers, early twenties.
BOYFRIEND, Jessie's ex, a future man's man, gets what he wants, early twenties.
DANIELLE, much like Jessie, with experience and remedies, late forties.

THE SCENE
The room of a modest suburban house. The entire play takes place in this one room. Now.

NOTES
A slash (/) indicates that the next character begins to speak over the current character speaking.

A dash (-) indicates the next character interrupts the current character speaking.

MOM and DANIELLE can be played by the same actress.
GALE and BOYFRIEND can be played by the same actress.
DAD and DIRECTOR can be played by the same

actor.

In JESSIE's bedroom, with her boldly femme bed and butch decorations, or the opposite. JESSIE is on it, with short hair and feminine clothes, or long hair and masculine clothes. Her parents are there, too, in their suits and proper outfits, or rather plain and suburban clothes. There's a ZAP ZAP sound.

JESSIE. Mom. Dad. Thank you for convening with me. I know that it's... challenging...to get the three of us together in one room, but now that I have you both here, I have something I want to say, or really something I *need* to say, because if I don't say it, I'll go crazy, so it's more of a *need* than a *want*, because even though I don't *want* to go crazy, I *need* to not go crazy. I gathered you here to tell you that I am... that I feel like a ball of yarn. Does that make sense? I feel like a ball of yarn that's been winding up for way too long, tumbling into this great enormous mass of yarn, curling around this...thing of mine, and it keeps getting bigger and bigger, the yarn that is, not the *thing*, the *thing* is the same and buried very deep, and I feel like a big fat giant ball of yarn that's ready to implode...*explode.* Or maybe the opposite? I feel like a ball of yarn that's been withering away for way too long, waning, slowly getting closer and closer to my...*thing*...and I'm almost naked and I think you can see it and everyone can see it, my *thing*, not the yarn, because like I said it's withering away, *waning*, but I'm not sure if you can see it, my *thing*, because I never asked and you haven't asked me, so I need to know if you know, and if you don't know then I want you to know, or else I'll go crazy, and I don't need or want that. I feel like a naked ball of yarn, sans the yarn. Does that make sense? *(Beat.)* Mom. Dad. I think I might be a...a *you know*...but I'm not entirely sure!

(Silence.)

MOM.   I have no words. *(Beat.)* Well, say something.

DAD.   Awful. Sick. Disappointing.

MOM.   Yes, indeed. Those words seem fitting.

DAD.   This must be rock bottom. I've heard of it before. It's quite dark.

MOM.   We shouldn't be here. This isn't right.

DAD.   This can't be our fault, can it?

MOM.   Teenagers do foolish things all on their own. This is certainly no result of our parenting.

DAD.   Should we send her to Father Gary?

MOM.   Don't involve the church. This is too embarrassing.

DAD.   God always gives second chances.

MOM.   You've always been a wishful optimist. I love that about you.

DAD.   You've always been an ambitious cynic. I love you even with that.

MOM.   Let's send her to rehab. Get her off of this awful addiction.

DAD.   She might resent us for that?

MOM.   Fine. Then it looks like we need to take this disaster into our own hands. A relief team, so to speak.

DAD.   Whatever you say, dear.

MOM.   Jessica. What did you say you were again?

JESSIE.   A...*you know.*

MOM.   Ah, that's right. *(Beat.)* New choice.

JESSIE.   Dad. Mom. I had this fleeting thought once, but then I had it again, and now it keeps coming back and haunting me, and I don't want it, but I think it's here to stay, to *haunt*, and it's not that I want it, but I have it--

DAD. New choice.

JESSIE. I'm...I'm a--

DAD AND MOM. New choice.

JESSIE. Who am I again?

MOM. Honey, I think she said regular! Did you hear that?

DAD. That's wonderful, dear, because I heard normal.

MOM. Perfect for our girl...regular AND normal!

DAD. Words from God / I might say.

MOM. That's right. Words from God, and God made you into the beautiful, regular, normal woman / that you are, Jessica.

DAD. A beautiful *average* woman, like everyone else!

MOM. You take after my mother, you really do. She was beautiful.

DAD. You take after mine, as well. She was average.

MOM. And beautiful.

DAD. And beautiful.

MOM. Our beauty is a gift.

DAD. A gift from God.

MOM. And that is why we must thank God / for our beauty.

DAD. Thank God that you are beautiful.

MOM. And regular.

DAD. And normal.

DAD AND MOM. Average.

JESSIE. Thanks, God.

DAD AND MOM. Thank you, God!

DAD. Tell God what you're thankful for, pumpkin.

(MOM and DAD vanish.)

JESSIE. Dear God, I am thankful for this little life of mine. It reminds me of the feeling that I get after waking up from a soft dream, or nightmare, a really awful nightmare, and I don't think about it, but I feel that I want to remember everything about it, the screaming sky, the disgusting sex, the forgetting self, and I feel that I want to remember all of it with my entire body, and I want it to fill me up like helium and float me away from this little life of mine, but in a moment, a moment that doesn't take up any space, if there is a word for that, in that untimely...that non-timely moment, I seem to forget the dream, everything, and I spend the rest of my day scratching at wallpaper trying to remember what it was, the components, the *stuff,* but I'm stuck in that feeling of hazy and wistful remembrances, where I really can't remember anything, until I forget that I ever dreamed at all, and that space between being asleep and being awake has melted into the air like a... / like a...like a...

(ZAP ZAP sound / MOM appears.)

MOM. Jessica. Jessica, wake up. Wake up.

JESSIE. Mom?

MOM. Jessica.

JESSIE. Was I...Was that all a...

MOM. Yes, and now it's lost in the sky with the cuckoo birds.

JESSIE. I have something to say. I've been sitting on this like an egg, and I think it's ready to hatch.

MOM. How about I take your eggs and scramble them up for a nice breakfast?

JESSIE. My egg! This is *my* egg.

MOM. You're right, this egg can never be mine...or this family's. You've grown it in a stranger's nest.

That's cuckoo business. It would be best to let it rot.

JESSIE. No! I've sat on it since I was twelve years old, stuck in the tree house with Gale Brown, during that fall snow-storm, the one where you couldn't find me, but I knew exactly where I was. I knew!

MOM. JESSICA WHITE! You stop that! *(Beat.)* Did you have a happy childhood, Jessica?

JESSIE. I did...Very happy.

MOM. Have I always given you what you wanted?

JESSIE. Yes. You have.

MOM. Did I ever hurt you?

JESSIE. No. You didn't.

MOM. Then please, shush. Just this...Just this.

(Beat.)

JESSIE. Oh, Mom. I wish I didn't need to talk. I wish I had nothing to say at all. I'm sorry.

MOM. Sorry about what?

JESSIE. Nothing, Mom. Nothing.

MOM. Jessica, you're thinking too much. You have to get out of your head. Let me sing you a lullaby. To help you wake up --

JESSIE. Wake up?

(MOM sings "Hush, Little Baby" / ZAP ZAP sound / DIRECTOR appears and interrupts.)

DIRECTOR. Hello? Is anyone in there? I need your slate please. Slate please. SLATE FOR ME--

JESSIE. My name is Jessie White!

DIRECTOR. Where are you from, Jessie?

JESSIE. Columbus, Ohio.

DIRECTOR. Where in Columbus?

JESSIE. Not exactly in Columbus. Right outside the city. In the suburbs.

DIRECTOR. How far from the city?

JESSIE. Two hours.

DIRECTOR. So, not from Columbus at all.

JESSIE. No, not Columbus.

DIRECTOR. Slate.

JESSIE. My name is Jessie White. I will be reciting a soliloquy from Shakespeare's *Hamlet*, playing the role of Hamlet.

"To be, or not to be: that is the question: Whether 'tis nobler in the mind / to suffer"--

DIRECTOR. Why don't we try something more appropriate.

JESSIE. Appropriate.

DIRECTOR. Good girl. Know any R&J?

JESSIE. I do.

"But soft, what light through yonder window breaks? It is the east, and Juliet is the sun.

Arise, fair sun, and kill the envious / moon"--

DIRECTOR. How about Juliet?

JESSIE. Yes.

"O Romeo, Romeo, wherefore art thou Romeo? Deny thy father and refuse thy name.

Or, if thou wilt not, be but sworn my love,

And / I'll"--

DIRECTOR. Having trouble?

JESSIE. What?

DIRECTOR. I want you to mean it when you talk about Romeo. Let me see how deeply in love you are with him.

JESSIE. "O Romeo, Romeo! wherefore art thou Romeo?"--

DIRECTOR. Stop. Stop. I don't buy it. Try to think about someone in your life who made you feel special, like you were the most important girl in the world. Have anyone like that?

(*GALE appears.*)

JESSIE. I did once. Oh, sure I did. I was important, but I was big too. I was the biggest *woman* in the

world. I could step on every little boy out there.
(*Kiss.*)
GALE. Squish.
DIRECTOR. Good. Take him.
JESSIE. Him?
DIRECTOR. And put him in front of you. (*GALE vanishes.*) Go.
JESSIE. "O Romeo, Romeo! Wherefore art thou Romeo? Deny thy father and refuse thy name"--
(*ZAP ZAP sound / BOYFRIEND appears.*)
BOYFRIEND. Let's have sex.
JESSIE. No!
DIRECTOR. Sorry?
JESSIE. Sorry.
"Or, if thou wilt not, be but sworn my love,
And I'll no longer be a Capulet."
BOYFRIEND. So have sex with me.
JESSIE. I'm not ready.
BOYFRIEND. New choice.
JESSIE. This is just our first date.
DIRECTOR. Try again.
JESSIE. "'Tis but thy name that is my enemy"--
BOYFRIEND. New choice.
JESSIE. I've never had sex with a man before.
DIRECTOR. You want the part, don't you?
JESSIE. I don't want to have sex with a man!
BOYFRIEND. Then why did I buy you dinner?
JESSIE. If I knew the words.
DIRECTOR. Times almost up.
JESSIE. Of course I want the part, but who would I be if I--
BOYFRIEND. New choice.
JESSIE. I do. I do want the part.
DIRECTOR. Good, because out there are thousands of girls just like you, but better looking,

stronger actors, bigger even. They could step on you--

BOYFRIEND. Squish--

DIRECTOR. But you gotta do what you gotta do to make it in this industry. Beat them to the... squish.

BOYFRIEND. Squish.

(DIRECTOR and BOYFRIEND gang up on both sides of her, sexually.)

JESSIE. Get off...get off of me!

(DIRECTOR vanishes / ZAP ZAP sound / MOM and DAD appear / BOYFRIEND persists.)

MOM. New choice.

JESSIE. I don't want you!

DAD. New choice.

JESSIE. It's just that I'm...I'm a--

BOYFRIEND. Come on. You're really trying to tell me that you don't want this? You'd be crazy to not want this! You're not crazy, are you? Oh God, I can't be with another crazy. There's this one girl, super hot, looks just like you, and you know how it goes. She's texting me all flirty and horny, so I give her the time of day and go over to her place. We bang, I leave, and that's all, or at least that's what I'm thinking. A year later I see her at this party, this crazy divorce party for some Mormon chick who got married off when she was fourteen. So, me and this girl are standing in this smoking circle together and she starts talking to me all friendly-like, so you know, I smile and am friendly back, I don't think much of it, but afterwards it feels like she's starting to follow me around, and when I go to try to take a piss, I have to wait in this stupidly long line to the bathroom, and she's right behind me. She could have gone anytime, but she deliberately waits right behind me. So we talk a little small talk, but I can

see that she wants more. It's the look she's giving me, that "I want to fuck you" kind of look, but I'm also confused because one of my pals warned me that she has a *girlfriend* now, this tiny dyke, so I don't know what to do. I decide that when it's my turn to go I'll leave the door slightly opened, as an invitation, you know, but she doesn't take it, probably because she's just shy. It must be hard for her to have those conflicting feelings with her new dyke and all, especially because she's high. So I thought I would help her out a little, so when it's her turn, before she can close the door, I push her in and lock it behind me, kinky-like, that way she knows I'm all in. She's just staring at me intensely with these huge eyes, backed into the wall, and it's pretty hot. Next thing I do is take off my pants and I am so turned on. I go right up to her, start kissing her neck, grabbing her boobs, and she doesn't try to stop me. She even moans a little, which is my cue to go, and it's hard to get in at first, especially because we have no lube and she's kind of dry because it's probably been a while for her, but I manage, and it feels pretty good. After a while though, I notice her looking kind of buggy, so I decide to pull out and play it cool. I go over to the toilet to take a piss again, like that's the reason I really pulled down my pants, even though I have no piss left, and I ask her if she's really a lez or not, and she's just nodding her head up and down like this dumb deer, so I zip up, open the door, and her dyke is there banging and crying. She runs out, and they leave. Next thing I find out, she tells everyone that I raped her. Crazy BITCH. She was the one leading me on! You're not crazy like her, right? You're not a--
JESSIE. Please. Please get off of me.

DAD. Dang it, but I want grand kids!

MOM. One day, dear. Right now we just need to help our little Jessica find her way. She's lost.

JESSIE. I am not lost.

BOYFRIEND. New choice.

JESSIE. I thought I knew, but maybe not.

BOYFRIEND. New choice.

JESSIE. If I were lost, would I ever know? Have I always been aimlessly heading the wrong way? Where am I *supposed* to go? Is it the ground? Have I been floating for so long that I forgot where the ground is? Or is it me that I've been floating away from? Floating / from this little life of mine...

MOM. Oh, you can't see right--

DAD. She's practically blind--

BOYFRIEND. What kind of blindy doesn't get confused here and there?

DAD. Luckily, blindness can be cured.

JESSIE. It can?

MOM. Lost girls can find their way home.

JESSIE. Lost...

BOYFRIEND. Everything can be / the way that it should be.

JESSIE. The way it should be.

DAD. Welcome, to Dr. Kim's electroconvulsive therapy!

MOM. Where your child can be cured.

BOYFRIEND. Zap zap! (*He plays with electrodes and they spark and make ZAP ZAP sounds.*)

MOM. Isn't that fun?!

JESSIE. Yes!

DAD. With a simple payment of twenty-five hundred American dollars--

BOYFRIEND. And your signature--

MOM. We can save your child!

JESSIE. I want to be saved!

(MOM and BOYFRIEND vanish.)

DAD. Now Jessica, what you're doing isn't... right. It's scary. *(He begins to strap JESSICA to her bed with electrodes.)* That's right, you are scaring your mother and me, and we need to fix that, because you should be our little pumpkin still, and not this...thing...that leaves you far from the girl you used to be. It makes me think that I'm going to lose you, but I can't lose my little pumpkin. So even though you're trying to...run away, I won't let you. We can get rid of this...thing...if we all work together as a family. As the saying goes, "You need to hit rock bottom before getting better," and this is rock bottom, Jessica. But God has presented us with a second chance, and we are taking it. This is the first step towards the real you. This is...good. This is good for you. At the end of the day your mother and I just want you to be happy, and we know that this is...right. This is right for the whole family. So get in there and do what you need to do to become our little pumpkin again.

(DAD vanishes. DANIELLE appears.)

DANIELLE. Hello, Jessica. I'm Dr. Danielle Kim. Please take a seat. I'm sorry to meet you under these circumstances. I'm sure that you're feeling embarrassed, but don't worry, it's normal for young women your age, and certainly most patients, as a matter of fact. It's not easy to come into my office and do this kind of work. It never is. But your parents paid good money, and I get paid that money, so we have a job to do. Before we begin the procedure, I have a few questions I must ask, to have something to compare our results to later on.

JESSIE. Okay.

DANIELLE. Have you ever been sexually attracted to another woman? *(Beat.)* Have you ever engaged in sexual acts with another woman? *(Beat.)* It's okay to not answer, these questions are just procedural. We both know why you're here. *(Beat.)* Do you believe that homosexuality is a mental disorder or certified form of neurosis?

JESSIE. I don't think so.

DANIELLE. Neither do I. Did you come here today of your own volition?

JESSIE. Not...exactly.

DANIELLE. I have your parents' signatures, but do you wish to undergo this procedure, Jessica?

JESSIE. I...uh...

DANIELLE. Try to not think. Just tell me what you're feeling.

JESSIE. I...I'm feeling like a ball of yarn, if that makes sense, that's been withering away since I was twelve, waning, slowly getting closer and closer, digging down to my...*thing*...and now, right now on this chair sitting in front of you, I feel like I am this *thing*.

DANIELLE. How does that feel, being this "thing"?

JESSIE. It feels... *(Beat.)* good.

DANIELLE. Does it now?

JESSIE. It feels good to know that you know, and to be with you, with your cognizant knowing. Even if you don't like it, and I don't want it, we both see it, are conscious of it, and acknowledge it. We're sharing the existence of this...thing.

DANIELLE. Would you like to keep this "thing" of yours, Jessica?

JESSIE. This thing...this thing isn't my friend. This thing hates me, and I hate it. We don't take care of each other...want each other...but in a strange way, we need each other to feel...myself, but myself is not...average. Why would I want that? A life of winding and waning and waiting for the moment I can feel like I'm normal...thinking that if I say it out loud I'll come back to the ground, steady, that I'll no longer live in that non-timed moment of coming out from a dream...and I'll finally be awake. I just want what every girl wants. I want to love my parents and think that they love me too. I want to get a job because I'm talented and I earned it. I want to be married one day and not get shot. I want to watch movies and cry at the end, not scream because they make me feel different. I want to be Snow White, Sleeping Beauty, and Rapunzel. When I was little I used to wish a Prince Charming would come and save me from this little life of mine, but you see, I never *wanted* that. If he saves me, I'll lose myself. I really will float away...

DANIELLE.   You see, Jessica, homosexuality is simple. Women like us, we either are or are not, and that is out of our control. What is in our control is whether we give our "thing" to them, and without this procedure of mine, I could teach you how to keep it *and* live with it. Acceptance is the first step on the path leading you towards yourself, and once you get there you can stand on the ground, firm, steady, with your thing snugged between your breasts, a somber smile of knowing, and fleeting thoughts that become dreams that become reality. A secret reality in a secret world full of secret women. They won't know our secret, though. We are going to tell them what they want to hear. This world...this America is not a space made for us, and it's not a space that's going to change for us. They'll make us think so, but that's just so they can catch us with their big butterfly nets and send us to offices like mine. You can't throw your space away though, Jessica. You just can't, because if you throw it away, then, who would you be? As long as we have our knowing, our acceptance, our shared existence, we can be us. It's not ideal, but it took many years for me to learn that it's the safest way. *(Beat.)* So Jessica, I must ask a few questions, to compare our results. Have you ever been sexually attracted to another woman?

JESSIE. No.

DANIELLE. Have you ever engaged in sexual acts with another woman?

JESSIE. No.

DANIELLE. Do you believe that homosexuality is a mental disorder or certified form of neurosis?

JESSIE. Yes.

DANIELLE. So do I. Did you come here today of your own volition?

JESSIE. Yes. I want to be here.

DANIELLE. I have your parents' signatures, but do you wish to undergo this procedure, Jessica?

JESSIE. Yes. I need this procedure to save myself.

DANIELLE. Now Jessica, just between you and me, for our knowing. Who are you?

(DANIELLE vanishes.)

JESSIE. I'm...I'm a-- Why is it that gay, bisexual, transgender, and queer are all adjectives, but lesbian is a noun? I am not lesbian, I am *a* lesbian. As if my sexuality is not a part of me, but all of me. Why is it that women have that, but men don't?

(GALE appears.)

GALE. Double standards.

JESSIE. Suppression.

GALE. Of?

JESSIE. Being human.

GALE. *Oppression.*

JESSIE. Who decided that women didn't need their own adjective? Are there any dictionaries made by women?

GALE. Should we be worried about who makes the dictionaries or who makes the words! Mm- hmm.

JESSIE. Words are nothing without dictionaries. Words aren't real without dictionaries. Words are just sounds without dictionaries.

GALE. But a word has to be a word before it can be put in a dictionary.

JESSIE. If I want to get a new word in the dictionary that could be lesbian's adjective, who would I talk to? Is there a position for this? You know what? This is men's fault. If they gave us our own word / we wouldn't--

GALE. If men GAVE us our own word? Like a stocking stuffer from Santa to us little girls? Thank you for the gift of identity, Santa. It's because of strong men like you that I have any semblance of who I am. Heaven knows that I could never decide for myself! You know why men didn't *give* us an adjective, Jess? Because God forbid we use an *adjective to describe ourselves*, to take ownership of our IDENTITY. To men, lesbian is a noun because it means our sexuality is shoved deep down our throats like a giant cock, and it's buried in there, growing out of our eyes and mouths and assholes like roses for them to sniff and tear apart. You think they care about us holding hands? Or if we ever get married? Or that I love you more than words can express? Hell no. Lesbian wasn't made for us, it was made for their porn and fantasies. Gay men evolved from sodomites because men, even gay men, have that power, but lesbians have always been lesbians, because we don't make the words. They do.

JESSIE. Then what am I, Gale?

GALE. How should I know?

JESSIE. What if I don't need a word...a dictionary? Maybe all I need are these feelings of mine...Maybe feelings aren't meant to be spoken at all...just felt.

GALE. As the proverb goes -- words ruin feelings. They are called feelings for a reason, you know. Not spokelings, or wordlings, but feelings. FEELINGS, for Christ's sake!

(Beat. Kiss. Beat. JESSIE takes off her electrodes.)

JESSIE. Gale, I get it now. These metal pieces in my hands, I know them. Even when I couldn't see them, they've been here, zapping me. I've absorbed all of this shock, and now I'm left here, feeling it vibrate through me like a virus. No doctor can save me, only I can save myself. I'm ready to save myself from them.

(DAD and MOM appear. They ignore GALE, who stays, staring.)

DAD. Jessica. Are you in there, pumpkin?

JESSIE. Yes. I'm here.

MOM. Are you back from the cuckoos?

JESSIE. Yes, Mom. They tried to take me, but I'm back now. I'm here to stay. In this space.

DAD. So the session...it worked?

JESSIE. I understand now.

MOM. We thought we almost lost you.

JESSIE. I'm right here. In front of you. Awake.

DAD. God gave us a second chance, Pumpkin. Thank you for taking it, but now--

MOM. We have to make sure--

DAD. To see if it's a fluke--

MOM. If you really are our little girl--
DAD. Jessica...
DAD AND MOM. Who are you?
JESSIE. I know, and I don't know if you know, but I don't care. My knowing isn't enough. Your acknowledgment isn't what I want. This world's accepting isn't what I need. I need to live in harmony, intimacy with myself. My thing. My thing isn't me, but I'm holding it in the palm of my hand, and I almost let her go, float away, but if I did that, I would have left too. I need to be me. I need my space to breathe, to pulse, to grow until it consumes this whole world. I am going to consume this world, and I will feel it inside of me, small like a child. Then I will give birth to it, and it will be different, it will be mine.
DAD. New choice.
JESSIE. There is no choice.
MOM. New choice.
JESSIE. The only choice is me.
DAD AND MOM. New choice.
(String appears in JESSIE's hand, seemingly from a loose ball of yarn. She tosses it.)
END OF PLAY.

Adoption
By Gillian Gurney and Jesse Nadel

Gillian Gurney

Gillian Gurney is from Los Angeles, CA and graduated from Harvard Westlake School in 2017 and is currently attending Boston University.

Jesse Nadel

Jesse Nadel is a rising sophomore at Yale University, where he is studying chemistry and economics. *Adoption* is the first and only play that Jesse has written (so far).

Adoption was part of the Playwrights Festival at Harvard Westlake, April 28 – 30, 2016. It was produced by Christopher Michael Moore and directed by Jona Yadidi. The technical director was Andrew Villaverde. The cast was as follows:

Michelle Jacobson............................Kayla Darini
Bryan Jacobson............................Erick Gredonia
Sandy..Talia Lefkowitz
Woman.......................................Kelly Riopelle

Adoption produced by Punk Monkey Productions at The Lounge Theatre in Hollywood, CA in May 2018. It was directed by Gwen Hillier. The lighting design was by Michael Massey. The board operator and stage manager was Jany Stehman. The cast was as follows:

Michelle Jacobson............................Laura Bohlin
Bryan Jacobson............................Travon McCall
Sandy..Tara Emerson

CHARACTERS:

BRYAN JACOBSON: Husband of Michelle Jacobson, recently married. High school stud, but Michelle truly wears the pants in their marriage. Just wants his wife to be happy.

MICHELLE JACOBSON: Wife of Brian Jacobson. High Strung, anxious, perfectionist.

SANDY: High school ex of Brian. Heart still damaged. Quite insane and still holds a grudge.

WOMAN: Works for the adoption company

Scene

BRYAN AND MICHELLE'S bedroom, and an office at an adoption agency.

Time

The present.

Scene 1: *BRYAN and MICHELLE's bedroom.*
At Rise, MICHELLE lies in bed, feeling anxious. Her husband, BRYAN, enters the room, Putting on his pajamas.

BRYAN. Honey, why do you always do this?
MICHELLE. I'm not doing anything, Bryan; I just like to be prompt.
BRYAN. You said to set the alarm for 6:30, when we have to get up at 8:00!
MICHELLE. Well, I'm not the one who presses the snooze button seven times!
BRYAN. Look, I know you're nervous, and I am

too, but I promise it's going to be fine.

MICHELLE. I don't know, honey.

BRYAN. Why don't we just take our minds off it for a while? I know something that will make you feel better.

MICHELLE. *(Ignoring Bryan.)* What if it just isn't meant to be?

BRYAN. Don't worry about it right now, ok? Let's just distract ourselves for a bit.

MICHELLE. Do you know what the capital of Slovenia is?

BRYAN. What?

MICHELLE. The capital of Slovenia, Bryan. They could easily ask us that tomorrow and you have to be prepared!

BRYAN. That isn't important right now, Michelle.

MICHELLE. But it is! Every single little thing is important.

BRYAN. Why don't we discuss this later? Do you want some tea? Or how about binge watching Downton Abbey. That always calms you down.

MICHELLE. Bryan, they need to be impressed. We don't have time to invest in T.V. right now!

BRYAN. They will be honey; we just have to be ourselves. That is the most important thing after all. What has gotten into you?

MICHELLE. Ok, I'm just going to say it...You drink two percent milk.

BRYAN. Yes...that is true. Now can we get back to-

MICHELLE. Do you understand how bad that is for you? Do you think they will be impressed tomorrow when they hear that?

BRYAN. Michelle, they aren't going to ask what milk I drink! They aren't going to ask any of this stuff. I think you just need to relax right now.

MICHELLE. You know what? You're right. I knew I forgot to take my Lunesta tonight! That commercial really is right. You always have a wonderful sleep on the --
BRYAN. *(Annoyed tone.)* Wings of Lunesta, I know.
MICHELLE. You are a lifesaver, Bryan. What would I do without you?
BRYAN. *(Sighs and hopelessly falls back onto the bed.)* The real question is, what will you ever do with me?
MICHELLE. What'd you say honey?
BRYAN. Nothing. Absolutely nothing.
END OF SCENE 1

> **Scene 2:** *Adoption Center.*
> *MICHELLE and BRYAN sit nervously on the couch in an office, which is facing a desk with stacks of paper and a computer. A woman pops in to notify them about their interviewer.*

WOMAN. Mr. and Mrs. Jacobson, someone will be right with you.
MICHELLE. Thank, God. We've been waiting for like an hour.
BRYAN. More like 5 minutes, but -
MICHELLE. *(Whispered.)* Shh! Bryan, I feel like we're being watched in here.
BRYAN. Ok, now you've lost it.
MICHELLE. No, seriously. I bet they are. I heard these decisions are made and discussed with a whole group of people, not just one interviewer. So I bet that whole group is looking at us right now and judging us.
BRYAN. I don't see why they'd do that.

MICHELLE. *(Whispered as she sits completely still.)* Don't move an inch. I bet it's in that computer over there.

BRYAN. Michelle, we can move around. How would they penalize us for that?

MICHELLE. Stop talking. Smile! Just smile, look friendly and approachable.

(Awkward moment with them forcing smiles.)

BRYAN. Ok, you know what? If you're so set on this idea of a camera being in the computer, then why don't I just try and -- *(Gets up from his seat and tries to walk over to the computer.)*

MICHELLE. *(Holds down Bryan forcefully.)* You can't do that! They'll see you!

(Sandy rushes in.)

SANDY. See what?

MICHELLE. How much I love that desk. Is that mahogany wood?

SANDY. I believe so…Anyway, Mr. and Mrs. Jacobson, I am so sorry. Today has been a crazy day. But, welcome to the Adoption Center! How are you guys?

MICHELLE. We're great! We woke up, drank our skim milk, and here we are.

SANDY. Well, that's good to hear! You know, I've always been a 2% milk kind of gal, but to each their own I guess.

BRYAN. Michelle, I TOLD YOU -

MICHELLE. That you love me so much? I know. *(To Sandy.)* He tells me every day. He is so loving, just like a father should be.

SANDY. That's great. Ok, let's get back to why we're all here today. So why do you two want to adopt?

MICHELLE. We feel that there is something

missing in our life. A void that only parenting could fill. You know, we just got married last year and -

SANDY. *(Obnoxiously.)* That's enough, thank you! Anyways, what do you two do for a living?

MICHELLE. Well, Bryan is a doctor. Saving lives is truly his passion.

SANDY. *(To Bryan.)* That's really admirable. What kind of medicine do you practice?

MICHELLE. He's a pediatric surgeon. It really is a great combination of his love of children and the practice of medicine.

SANDY. That's so sweet! What hospital do you work at?

MICHELLE. *(Continuing to answer for him.)* Um, you know...the one...Grey Sloane Memorial Hospital.

SANDY. That's the hospital from television series, Greys Anatomy.

MICHELLE. See, that's what you think. But, it's actually based off the real hospital where he works.

BRYAN. Ok, I can't listen to this - I'm actually a telemarketer for a toothpaste company. It's great. I get to call and talk to so many people a day. And only a few of them yell profanity at me!

MICHELLE. Did I say pediatric surgery? I meant telemarketing. I get those two mixed up all the time.

SANDY. I don't know quite know how to respond to that. *(Pause.)* Ok, let's see...do you guys speak any languages other than English?

(In unison.)

BRYAN. No

MICHELLE. Yes!

SANDY. This is a very interesting dynamic you two have going here. But I'm sure you two are just nervous. That's common. Just try to answer these questions with complete honesty and everything will be fine. Alright, next. Michelle, how do you like being married?

MICHELLE. *(Touching Bryan's knee.)* I can honestly say that he's the best thing that's ever happened to me. He's funny, smart...I really don't know what I would do without Bryan.

BRYAN. Honey, that's so sweet. *(Putting his hand on top of hers.)*

(There's a long pause as Sandy is starring into space, thinking.)

MICHELLE. Are you alright?

SANDY. What? Oh, of course, I'm alright! I was just thinking...Bryan Jacobson, is it?

MICHELLE. That's right! He's actually a third generation of -

SANDY. I honestly do not care. I don't need your sales pitch. *(Mischievously.)* But here's a good question, have either of you ever experimented with any substances?

MICHELLE. Of course not!

SANDY. And not you, Bryan?

BRYAN. Absolutely not

SANDY. Not even at Austin Callahan's seventeenth birthday party?

BRYAN. Ok, that was one puff, and I have never done it since, and...Wait, how do you...

SANDY. Bryan, I truly am offended you do not recognize your girlfriend from the majority of junior year of high school. I mean it's okay, of course; I'm so over you anyway. It's just I thought you would remember me...

BRYAN. *(An awkward pause.)* Sandy! Of course, it's just been a while -

SANDY.   Really? Because I feel like it was just yesterday I caught you cheating with Rose Burns after school that one Wednesday.

MICHELLE. Bryan! You never told me that!

BRYAN.   I didn't tell you that because I didn't cheat! Sandy, I had broken up with you earlier that week!

SANDY. *(To Michelle.)* I'm surprised he's lied to all these years. You know, once a cheater, always a cheater. Run while you can!

MICHELLE.   Bryan you broke this poor woman's heart!

BRYAN. Michelle, honey, -

SANDY.   I don't have time to listen to your senseless argument! Let's move on. Seems like someone already has.

BRYAN. I feel as though this is unfair.

SANDY. It most certainly is. Anyway, I now have some questions specifically for Bryan. What is the capital of Slovenia?

MICHELLE.   *(Looking at Bryan.)* What did I tell you?!

BRYAN. *(Ignoring Michelle.)* Is that even relevant?

SANDY. No not at all, but I do expect an answer in the next five seconds.

BRYAN.   I don't know, but I know that Michelle does.

MICHELLE. *(Awkward pause, feeling embarrassed for not knowing. Sarcastically.)* Yeah, of course, I do! Um...Ljubljana?

SANDY. Is that your final answer?

MICHELLE. Wait! No, no. Bryan, I know that's not right. Say something else!

BRYAN. Gosh, um...Abu Dhabi?

SANDY. Well, as well as that being in a completely

separate country, Abu Dhabi is also on a completely different continent. So you are wrong on many accounts. And ironically Michelle, you were correct. Seems as though Bryan is hard to trust.

BRYAN.   I would've gotten it right, it's just I'm nervous! You said that was common. Remember?

SANDY.   Do you know when I was nervous, Bryan? When I had to go alone to junior prom, because my boyfriend abandoned me. Why didn't you take me to prom?

BRYAN.   Sandy, we weren't together when prom happened!

SANDY.   And your point is?

BRYAN.   *(Starts to speak but Sandy cuts him off.)* My point -

SANDY.   And do you remember that one time you were late?

BRYAN.   Late for what?!

SANDY.   To pick me up! You had football practice and you said it ended at four when it really ended at four-fifteen. I had to wait fifteen minutes in the cold!

BRYAN.   Oh my god, this is insane. I don't think that happened, but even if it did, it's fifteen extra minutes!

SANDY.   Bryan, if I were you, I wouldn't talk back right now. You're not exactly in the position to, that is, if you want to adopt.

MICHELLE.   *(Staring incredulously at their argument.)* I would like to request for a different interviewer.

SANDY.   *(Without missing a beat.)* I'm sorry, but unfortunately, all of the others are in other interviews right now.

MICHELLE.   You didn't even check!

SANDY. That is true.

MICHELLE. Ok Sandy, I do love making fun of my husband just as much as you do, but this doesn't seem right. Look, he's not a doctor, I know, but he is my husband, and he's a great guy, an amazing one, actually, and just because you dated him in high school, doesn't give you the right to talk to him this way! He's my husband now, so I suggest you treat him like a normal client. This just isn't fair!

SANDY. Life isn't fair, Michelle. Read a book. You know, I really do advise you to find another husband. I'm really starting to question your intelligence.

BRYAN. Ok, Sandy, that's enough. I get it. You're still not over me, and that's ok. I get it, and you can be mad at me. That definitely wasn't one of my finest moments, but you have no right to talk to my wife like that. She doesn't deserve to be treated like this. Either act professionally or we're leaving!

SANDY. Fine, we'll see if you two are able to adopt now!

(*SANDY scrambles together papers and exits, leaving MICHELLE and BRYAN sitting alone.*)

BRYAN. Well, now I guess we'll have to give up on that dream.

MICHELLE. What are you talking about?

BRYAN. That was absolutely awful. There's no way she's going to allow us to adopt.

MICHELLE. Bryan, we did exactly what you said to do. We were ourselves! Even if that did involve us yelling...but that's beside the point. If we don't get this opportunity, we'll just keep looking.

BRYAN. You're right, honey. What would I do without you?

MICHELLE. *(Joking.)* Probably not be able to make a living for yourself, starve -

BRYAN. Hey! That's not the point, but thank you.

MICHELLE. For what?

BRYAN. Just for being you. *(Holds Michelle's hand.)* Now, let's just hope being ourselves is enough.

(SANDY walks back in holding papers.)

SANDY. *(In an extremely sarcastic tone.)* I have discussed with the other administrators, and to my dismay, you two have passed.

BRYAN. How? We were such a mess!

SANDY. How? I don't understand this, but they somehow liked how you two stood up for each other. Called it *(Air quotes.)* endearing or something.

BRYAN. Well, this is incredible! Honey, we are going to become parents. Can you imagine what our life is going to be like?

MICHELLE. I know! It almost doesn't seem real that we'll be like all those couples we see all the time, but I can't wait. It is a lot of responsibility though...

BRYAN. But we're ready. I know we are.

SANDY. Will you two just calm down. It's just a freaking dog! You two can handle it. But please, don't ever have children.

(A dog barks as lights fade.)
END

Bud, Wiser

By Michael Narkunski

Michael Narkunski

Michael Narkunski is expected to graduate Summer 2018 with his MFA in Creative Writing and Literature at Stony Brook University, where he divided his energy between prose and scriptwriting. His personal essays have appeared in *Out*, *Narratively*, *Hippocampus Magazine*, *Full Grown People*, and two LGBT anthologies, while his plays have had readings and performances presented in NYC by Dixon Place, Snorks & Pins, Left Hip, Naked Angels' Tuesdays@9, and The Playground Experiment. He was a finalist in the Film Daily competition for his TV pilot script, *Ezekiel Bound*. BFA: NYU Tisch.
Visit him at: www.michaelnarkunski.com

Bud, Wiser was originally produced by Punk Monkey Productions at The Lounge Theatre in Hollywood, CA in May 2018. It was directed by Dean Bruggeman. The lighting design was by Michael Massey. The board operator and stage manager was Jany Stehman. The cast was as follows:

Freddy..Lee Pollero
Ryan..Phil Biedron

CHARACTERS:

> **FREDDY:** Male, 30, gay, somewhat effeminate, sensitive, and mentally tortured
> **RYAN:** Male, 30, gay, masculine, sporty, blustery, and mentally free
>
> *Place*
> *A gay bar*
>
> *Time*
> *Winter, 2017*
>
> *FREDDY, 30, sits with a Budweiser bottle at a gay bar. He's been waiting a long time and has already had quite a few. He addresses the invisible "bartender."*

FREDDY. You know what my theory is? It's that people like to say "Bud." "I'll take a Bud..." "I'll grab a Bud..." "Give me a Bud..." It's really like they're asking for a friend, a pal, an amigo, like, "Sure, a deep, satisfying, mutually beneficial relationship? I guess, if you must, why not?" ...That's what's ideal for most people, I think. How they like to treat others: casually, like something easy they're just entitled to. Especially our kind, my God, we're the worst! (Well actually, you're working in a...but I don't know if you're a...) But you know what I mean. All our random hook-up-this and our open relationship-that. And now? PrEP?! It's like no one wants to pay the price anymore! To do the work! But we're all forgetting one crucial thing: there's absolutely nothing-- nothing in this whole godforsaken world you ever get for free... *(FREDDY sits in brief reverie, then jolts.)* What? Oh, sorry, sorry! *(Getting cash out.)* Here you go. And sure...get me a Bud. *(Shaking his head.)* Genius fucking branding. *(He takes a swig. Then waves his hand.)* No, no, on second thought, forget it. I'm sorry. I'm just nervous. Ha, was that out loud? No, I should stop. I should even maybe go. Why torture myself? *(He really thinks about that.)*

(To himself.) Am I? *(To bartender.)* What? Oh, I'm waiting for...this guy. We used to be friends. *(Singing.)* "A long time ago / We used to be friends..." you know that song? That like, describes us. ...Wow, you're fuckin' stupid--I mean--not you! I mean me, I mean *(He listens.)* Yes, "cut off," that's also a good description of us. *(Pause.)* Yeah, ha ha, I get it...

(He takes another swig, and slowly, drunkenly, bends over to grab his somewhat effeminate coat. As he does so, RYAN, 30, creeps up behind, finger-gun in his back.)

RYAN. Put the faggot jacket down and get yourself another round!

FREDDY. ...Ryan.

RYAN. Non, non, non, c'est Ree-on! "Ryan" was my hetero slave name!

(FREDDY finally turns around. He tries to keep it together.)

FREDDY. Uhh...ha...I...did you want to...?

RYAN. Screw you til you scream obscenities in languages you never thought you knew? Nah, not tonight, Freddykins. Let's go slow. I will have a seat though! *(RYAN sits down with a giddy smile. He sees FREDDY is freaked out.)* Oh, shit. Sorry, Freddy. Rebecca told you, right? This isn't surprise of the century, is it?

FREDDY. No, no, she told me that you came out.

RYAN. Oh OK, phew.

FREDDY. She told me. And Facebook told me. And Twitter. And Grindr...

RYAN. Just checking. You looked even whiter than usual!

FREDDY. Than usual?

RYAN.   Well, you know...than you used to. *(Awkward pause.)* So, uh, how's your life been? You were always a smart guy. I bet you've done some sweet things! Wrote a few unpublished novels, taught abroad in South Korea, volunteered...

(RYAN laughs. FREDDY's eyes narrow.)

FREDDY. It's...yeah, it's been fine. You're actually frighteningly close.

RYAN. Well, uh, that stuff's all good.

FREDDY. ...And...you?

RYAN. Oh, you know, I keep active. Do my shitty market analysis to pay those electric and CrossFit bills, but been getting into skydiving actually, if you can believe it.

FREDDY. Skydiving...huh...

RYAN. Yep. Don't want to sound like some 100-jump-wonder wannabe, but my number's definitely getting up there! Even training to be an instructor soon!

FREDDY. Great. Great, that's um--

RYAN. Hey, remember when I couldn't even keep in my lunch on the freakin' candlestick ride? Blehhhhhhhh!!!!!

(Silence. FREDDY stares into RYAN's eyes, intensely.)

FREDDY. You know, it took a lot for me to come.

RYAN. OK... *(Smiling.)* I cum almost instantly.

FREDDY. This isn't a joke...this isn't a joke...

(FREDDY sits down and really seems broken now. RYAN looks around, confused. He starts to back off.)

RYAN. Um, OK, maybe this wasn't the best idea. We haven't seen each other in awhile, really since grade school, and we probably just don't, um, gel anymore, despite...But that's totally fine, man! Don't worry about it, we don't have to force it. I'll just, ya know, see you around the bars or something...

(He pats FREDDY on the back and starts to exit.)

FREDDY. *(Seething.)* So you're just gonna go again? Huh, motherfucker?

(RYAN stops, turns, then goes toward FREDDY, close.)

RYAN. Listen man, I don't know your problem, but you don't want to get rough with me. I'm a big guy.

FREDDY. *(Knowingly.)* Yeah, I remember.

RYAN. What's that supposed to mean?

FREDDY. I can't believe this. I mean, I thought you'd maybe have some kind of apology for...that night. And if not, my therapist said that you might show some kind of remorse, or, I don't know, humility. But you're acting like, like, nothing even happened!

RYAN. Happened? What? Look, you're really weirding me out, man. I mean, I guess I'm sorry I didn't know sooner for you, and boy, for a lot of reasons not involving you. But nothing I did should warrant a reaction like this. I go to therapy, too, man. I know my rights.

FREDDY. More jokes...

RYAN. Hey, I'm not kidding! You think I haven't been through the wringer? I wasn't like you. It's harder for more masculine guys like me. Relationships with googly-eyed girlfriends you don't care anything about, teammates who don't know who you really are..

FREDDY. Apparently you don't even know who you really are.

RYAN. Yes. I do.

FREDDY. Well, then fill me in. I'd love to hear.

RYAN. Freddy, I already told you that night....

(RYAN slowly, strangely, takes off his shirt, then faces the audience, throws open his arms and screams:) I'm the king of the world!

(FREDDY jumps up off his stool. They are both back in childhood, at RYAN's house, excited and playing Titanic.)

FREDDY. Yeahhhhh! Man, that movie was so good!

RYAN. Me and my mom are going again next weekend!

FREDDY. Cooool.

RYAN. Yeah. *(Pause.)* I'm the king of the world!!

FREDDY. I'm the king of the world!!

(They keep shouting it and running around. RYAN grabs a water gun out of his pocket and shoots at FREDDY.)

RYAN. Bang, bang, bang! Rose's boobies will belong to me!

FREDDY. Wait, don't! Seriously, my mom will kill me if my clothes get wet and I get sick again!

(RYAN aims his gun.)

RYAN. Then take your shirt off for once. You never do.

FREDDY. Should I?

RYAN. Yeah, come on. It's fun!

(FREDDY thinks about it, then takes off his shirt.)

FREDDY. OK, shoot.

(RYAN smiles. He throws his gun down and attacks FREDDY. He screams.)

RYAN. Now we can finally do WWF!! Hulk Hogan vs. Shawn Michaels!

(FREDDY is no match for RYAN.)

RYAN. And Hulk goes for the half-nelson! *(As Hogan.)* "What are you gonna do about it, Brother? Huh? What are you gonna do?"

FREDDY. *(Struggling.)* I'm... I'm gonna...

(He reaches back and peels RYAN's hand off him, then turns around, gets him restrained, and impulsively kisses him. RYAN lets him momentarily, then pushes him off.)

RYAN. Ew! What are you doing? *(Pause.)* Homo! You homo!

(FREDDY quickly puts his shirt back on, as does RYAN.)

FREDDY. I thought it was OK. I-I thought we were buddies...

RYAN. Not anymore! Get out of my house! Get out, you...you freak! I'm telling everybody! Everybody! Do you hear me?? *(While RYAN repeats, they slowly, hypnotically, take their places back in the present.)* Do you hear me? Do you hear me? Do you hear me, Freddy?

FREDDY. What? Yeah...yeah.

RYAN. You zoned out a little there.

FREDDY. I just...I can't believe that's how you remember it.

RYAN. Sure. I mean, I liked it--the kiss--I think, but, you know my family, I just couldn't deal and flipped out. It's not like I really told anybody. We did blood brothers! We watched Beetlejuice like twenty-five times! ...Why? What do you remember?

FREDDY. Um. It doesn't matter. *(Changing the subject.)* So, are you too young to be called a "daddy"?

RYAN. Come on! I'm real interested. What was so different??

FREDDY. Listen, I think it's time for me to head home. I live back with my mom again while I finish graduate school--and she worries if I'm too late.

RYAN. OK. Fine. That's fair. *(Coughs.)* Scapegoat.

FREDDY. What did you say?

RYAN.   Nothing...just...well...you always did blame everything on your mom growing up. You could never sleep over, never play chicken at the pool, everything was always "my mom said," "my mom worries" when really, we all knew...it was just you.

FREDDY. This is why you wanted to meet? To taunt me?

RYAN. No! I wanted to reconnect with my old best friend, who I thought would be happy to see me, and ecstatic that I'm finally being my authentic self!

FREDDY. Authentic self...right...

RYAN. Right. And I'm sorry you've turned so bitter, but that doesn't mean you have to shit all over my growth just because you're not getting laid or whatever. Just because you're being some evasive, cowardly...

(RYAN stops himself.)

FREDDY. What? Cowardly what?

RYAN. ...Pussy.

(RYAN laughs to himself. Then gets steely.)

FREDDY. We did just come from Titanic, that part's true. And we were in your basement, but, well, as you know... *(FREDDY slowly pulls out handcuffs from his pocket.)* We weren't doing the gun scene.

(RYAN suddenly charges, takes the handcuffs and locks FREDDY's hands around a "pipe." They are ten again.)

FREDDY. Ryan! Ryan! Stop!

RYAN. I know you're a little faggot boy.

FREDDY. You're acting crazy!

RYAN. You had a boner for Jack through the whole movie.

FREDDY. No! Gross! I didn't!

RYAN. I'm gonna show you what happens to little faggot boys. You can be just like Jack!

(RYAN exits, comes back quickly with a "heavy" bucket.)

FREDDY. Ryan! Ryan, no! Stop! Stop! I'm gonna drown!

RYAN. "I'm gonna drown!" You shut up! Shut up...Or I'll make you shut up.

FREDDY. Help! Help!!

(RYAN chokes FREDDY, still on the ground.)

RYAN. Stop! Stop and take your punishment!

(He slowly pours the "water" on FREDDY, who gasps and writhes.) You're a faggot! You're disgusting! You don't take your shirt off when we play because you're a girl! You don't want to play tackle football because you don't want to get a boner. Well, here, get a big boner now! Get a boner, I said!

FREDDY. *(Struggling for breath.)* Please! Please! I'll be good. I won't be that way. I'll change. I promise. I promise!

RYAN. What do you promise?

FREDDY. I promise...I'll like girls...

(RYAN kicks FREDDY. He cries.)

RYAN. What will you do to them?

FREDDY. I'll...kiss them.

(RYAN kicks.)

RYAN. What will you do?!

FREDDY. I'll...fuck them...I'll fuck them...I swear.

(RYAN laughs.)

RYAN. With your little boner, Freddykins?? Are you sure??

FREDDY. *(Over RYAN's laughs.)* Just let me go! Let me go! Let me GO! *(He breaks free from the "pole" and*

flings himself downstage of RYAN, curls up in a fetal position.) Let me go...let me go...let me go...
(While FREDDY repeats, RYAN goes to Freddy, steadily again hypnotically, takes off FREDDY's handcuffs, puts them away, and leans over.)
RYAN.   Freddy. Freddy, you're fine. People are looking. We're gonna get booted. Stop...
(FREDDY blinks, snapping out of it.)
FREDDY.   OK...I'm OK...
RYAN.   Good...good...Listen, um, is there someone--someone I can call? I don't think you're in a condition to be alone, and I have to really get--
FREDDY.   *(Resigned.)* You deny it.
(RYAN freezes. FREDDY gets up.)
RYAN.   Um.
FREDDY.   Just say so. You deny it. I can see that you want to.
RYAN.   ...It's a sick story, man.
FREDDY.   Yes. It's also what you did.
RYAN.   *(Recounting.)*   I chained you up like a dog. At 10 years old. And water-boarded you. At 10 years old. And I hit--
FREDDY.   You kicked me. Over and over. And I went home and told my mother that my brother did it when she saw the bruises, because I couldn't let the real reason be found out--not yet.
RYAN.   Where did I get the handcuffs? How did my parents not come help you from the screaming?
FREDDY.   I asked myself that for years. I was hoping you'd have some answers. Any answers.
(Pause.)
RYAN.   You've built it up, man. I don't know what to say. I'm sorry.
FREDDY.   Don't say you're sorry for what I "think" happened. That's not the kind of-- You know--I'll

just deal with this all myself. I knew you might be gay, self-hating. Not then, obviously, but it had been a possibility--

RYAN. With your therapist.

FREDDY.   Yes. When I gained some perspective. And now that you're out, it makes a lot more sense. Confirmed sense. There's still the damage that was done--the confusion...humiliation. For years. The loss of my best friend. And now his denial I'll have the pleasure of spending entire paychecks processing. But at least I've learned my lesson--to let sleeping pit bulls lie, and I can just get out of here before I really lose. My. Shit.

(FREDDY leaves to go, but RYAN grabs him.)

RYAN.   Wait. There--there is something familiar. About it. Maybe there was something that--

FREDDY.   It's fine! You really don't need to play this game! Please let me--

RYAN.   Wait! Just wait. I really. I'm trying. It's just...it's remote. Like the drop zone of a jump. Let me just...this will take...yep, this will take some precision landing.

(RYAN entrances himself, slowly pantomimes putting on a jumpsuit, a backpack.)

FREDDY. What is this...

RYAN.   I'm strapping in. Now I'm going up...now tracking my wind line...

FREDDY.   Ryan. Stop. This isn't funny. I'm not going to be made a mockery of by someone who was the face of my nightmares for years and years. Someone who can't even--

(RYAN pretends to rip back the plane door.)

RYAN.   And blue skies! Blue, blue skies! A beautiful day for a tandem jump into the quarter-sized target of the past! Weather perfect. Clouds perfect. All that's left is a nutcase to embrace them, and a bigger one to follow.

(FREDDY steps toward RYAN, red-faced.)

FREDDY.   Are you mentally deranged? Are you goddamn cracked? Huh??

RYAN. *(Low, serious.)* Listen, you can go home and sulk, Freddy. Keep living vaguely in your trauma. And maybe you'd have every right. But this is tricky business, this memory stuff. And I know the best way to attack it, the best way for a clear head, real perspective...is to go airborne. *(RYAN comes toward, touches FREDDY by the waist.)* Now...do you trust me?

FREDDY.   I...I...used to. Before that night? I used to worship the ground you walked on.

RYAN.   I need you to go back to that. Despite what happened. Despite all your well-founded fears.

FREDDY.   I want to, I want to so badly, but--

RYAN.   And we're out! Quick: box-man! *(RYAN, in a flash, gets behind FREDDY and guides him into the "box-man" position, arms and legs out.)* There we go. We're doing it, Freddy.

FREDDY.   Uh, what are we doing??

RYAN.   Free-falling! Do ya feel it? The force?? Feel it in your guts??

FREDDY.   I--I don't...Um...I think...?

RYAN.   Not "I think." Do you feel it? Like when we were little, playing pretend?

FREDDY.   I...feel it. I feel it.

RYAN.   What do you feel?

FREDDY.   I feel the rush. My mind going blank.

RYAN.   Great. Watch out--sky shark!!

FREDDY. What??

RYAN.   Another plane! No, no, it's the handcuffs from your memory! Look!

FREDDY. I...uh...

RYAN. Do you see it?? Concentrate!

FREDDY. Yeah... I, I see it!

RYAN. What does it look like?

FREDDY. Oh…Oh...I don't know. Like handcuffs!

RYAN. It's hurdling towards us! Are they silver? Are they real?

FREDDY. They're, uh, from a magic set! They're for kids--I--

RYAN. Your old magic set?

FREDDY. Yes. In my house. I wanted to have power. I wanted to disappear when I wanted.

RYAN. Well, there's no hiding now, buddy. Hold tight, going for the de-arch! *(RYAN takes them out of box-man, into a de-arched position.)* Awesome form! Oh shit, to the left, another, it's our kiss!!

FREDDY. There was no kiss! You invented that! I want to land!

RYAN. Why? If it wasn't real or even if it was, what's to fear??

FREDDY. I--I don't—nothing. *(Looking closely, realizing.)* There's nothing to fear.

RYAN. It's just a kiss.

FREDDY. That's right.

RYAN. You knew how I looked at you back then. You knew I'd like it.

FREDDY. That's right.

RYAN. It wasn't your fault how I reacted.

FREDDY. No...no. It wasn't. And...and it wasn't yours either...

RYAN. Huh?

FREDDY. Look, Ryan, through the clouds. It's the other kids at school! It's The Chain!!

RYAN. Who the--oh! You mean--

FREDDY. The rest of our friend-group! Jared,

Daniel, Travis. Remember? We called ourselves The Chain. We wouldn't be broken!

RYAN. I forgot! I see them! I see their George Clooney Caesar-cuts and JNCO jeans!!

FREDDY. What else?

RYAN. They're talking about us--making fun of us for spending so much time together. I--I see myself wanting to show them they were wrong...

FREDDY. So you told them. You told them--

RYAN. I told them the truth. That you kissed me. And they...went over to your place...and...they... they...

(FREDDY looks back at RYAN, now the despondent one.)

FREDDY. Pull the 'chute, Ryan.

(RYAN doesn't. Instead, he drops his form, pauses, then drifts over to the bar, lost in thought. FREDDY stands, deeply processing. Touches his wrists, shakes his head. Eventually, he looks over to RYAN. Rubs his neck.)

FREDDY. *(Deeply confused.)* I'm, I'm sorry that--

RYAN.   Don't apologize. You shouldn't ever apologize to me... *(Pause. FREDDY walks over to RYAN, hangs.)* They did everything you said. Didn't they? It was why you went to the far away middle school after that summer. Why we never saw you outside in the neighborhood anymore. While we biked around shouting at the top of our lungs...

(FREDDY shrugs.)

FREDDY. Boo hoo. Why would I want to hang out with you losers, anyway? More time to cultivate my apparently overactive imagination!

RYAN. Not overactive. It was my fault. It was me. In a way...I betrayed you. And they took you and...it must have killed you.

FREDDY. You preserved yourself. Plenty of gay

kids do. And look, it worked. You're here now. …You made it.

RYAN.   Yeah. Sure. Twenty years and two shell-shocked fiancées later. I made it.

(FREDDY tries to smile.)

FREDDY.   If you spend the next twenty beating yourself up for all the mistakes you made in the closet to please our heterosexual overlords, you'll be fifty before you reach the emotional maturity of Kanye West.

RYAN.   Look, I don't need an excuse for my actions.

FREDDY.   You mean a scapegoat.

RYAN.   Right, I'm not a little bitch!!

(FREDDY's stunned, then exhales in disbelief. Shakes his head, and picks up his coat, and gets close to the exit. RYAN looks over his shoulder. He forces it out.) Thanks for indulging me! …With the skydive.

(FREDDY stops. Pause.)

FREDDY.   Well, "You jump, I jump, right?"

(RYAN sadly chuckles.)

RYAN.   That…that was a really good scene…I so love Kate Winslet….

FREDDY.   I know. Hey, did you see Revolutionary Road? When she and Leo reunited?

(RYAN turns.)

RYAN.   Dude, did you see Little Children?

(FREDDY turns.)

FREDDY.   Oh my God, so underrated!

RYAN.   I'm sayin'…hands-down the best suburban hell of all the suburban hell movies.

(FREDDY walks himself back to him.)

FREDDY.   I have the script signed.

RYAN.   *(Wowed.)* Stop.

FREDDY.   I had it bad for that movie. I got the writer, the director, and the old--

RYAN. Not the old lady...! She was--
RYAN AND FREDDY. So good!!!
(They look at each other. Have a moment. RYAN stares.)
RYAN. I...owe beer.
FREDDY. Um, huh?
RYAN. "Stupid hurts." Skydiving motto. I didn't pull the parachute. When you do something dumb in the air that can get everyone slaughtered--you owe your posse beer.
FREDDY. Sounds...balanced.
RYAN. Yeah, so what you drinkin'?
FREDDY. Just cheap.
RYAN. If you insist. Hey, bartender, get this guy a 'weiser. Actually, make it two 'weisers.
(Beat.)
FREDDY. Wait, "'weiser"? You don't say, "bud"? "Get me a Bud"?
RYAN. Eh, nah. I've always hated that phrase. It always sounded so...freakin' entitled! *(FREDDY stares, then laughs. Laughs more.)* What?...What did I say? What?
(He can't stop, as RYAN looks on, semi-amused. FREDDY's doubled over, laughing at it all.)
End of play

.

American Pie

By Rebecca Katz

Rebecca Katz

Rebecca is a senior studying Journalism and Political Science at the University of Southern California. She has been writing as long as her hand was big enough to hold a pen -- beginning with short stories, and moving to one act plays, personal essays, and long-form journalism.

American Pie was part of the Harvard Westlake Playwrights Festival, April 25-27, 2014 in North Hollywood, CA. It was produced by Christopher Michael Moore and directed by Noah Bennett. The technical director was Andrew Villaverde. The cast was as follows:

Jackson Bailey...........................Carlos Guanche
Jenny Slater.................................Aiyana White

American Pie was produced by Punk Monkey Productions at The Lounge Theatre in Hollywood, CA in May 2018. It was directed by James Elden. The lighting design was by Michael Massey. The board operator and stage manager was Jany Stehman. The cast was as follows:

Jackson Bailey..........................Damon McKinnis
Jenny Slater....................................Sami Henry

CHARACTERS:

JACKSON BAILEY: Seventeen. Has a soft, charming, Texas drawl which makes everything he says feel very real and personal. Plays football for the Clovis Cougars making him well known and admired in the small town, has a love for the game and the town like no other.

JENNY SLATER: A smart, driven, adventurous seventeen year old. A girl too big for the town she's living in; a dreamer. Also has a soft, deep Texas drawl.

SETTING: 1983. A small beat up white house in a tiny town - Clovis, Texas. A torn, used, large leather suitcase sits on the side of the porch steps.

AT RISE: JACKSON BAILEY walks out of his house, slamming the front screen door, holding a laundry basket full of footballs. He stands outside of his house holding a beaten up brown leather football in hand. He begins to pantomime a game.

JACKSON. *(Whispers, milking it in the voice of an announcer.)* Folks, it's all come down to this for the 1983 Texas High School State Championship. We're here at the Cotton Bowl and there's time for one more play. The Longview Bobcats came into the game as heavy favorites and ready to stomp all over our own Clovis Cougars. But something happened after the half and that something was Jackson Bailey! He just about single-handedly put us right back in this gosh-darned game. Every decent man and woman in Clovis are on their knees prayin' that the boy has one more bit of magic left in him. The ball's snapped, Bailey fades back. That's a long spiral. Wow, I don't know anyone who can throw quite like Jackson Bailey. (*Jackson smiles to himself.*) Hell, I don't even see a receiver. Holy bass boat! There's Jackson Bailey, again! He dives! He's in the end zone! Touchdown! Bust my britches! That is the greatest play I've ever seen. The Cougars win! The cougars win! God bless Jackson Bailey!

(*JACKSON lays on the stage with the ball outstretched in his arms, eyes closed, out of breath, heart pounding, smile on his face. JENNY SLATER, leans against her front screen door, and begins a slow clap. JACKSON opens his eyes, looking up at her, unaware he was being watched by his neighbor.*)

JENNY. (*Poking fun at him.*) Wow, are you really Jackson Bailey?! I knew you were talented, but who knew you could play so many positions at the same time!

JACKSON. They're lots of things you don't know bout me, Jenny Slater.

(*SFX of parents hollering at each other and something shattering from within JACKSON's house. JENNY glances over at him with a knowing look.*)

JENNY. They fightin' again?

JACKSON. Sun come up today?

(*She pulls out a beat up Walkman with some headphones, popping in a cassette.*)

JENNY. This is probably better to listen to.

JACKSON. Thanks.

JENNY. You know what they say, the music will save your soul.

(*He flashes his signature crooked smile, briefly.*)

JACKSON. American Pie. A classic.

JENNY. It's one of my favorites. I've always

thought it was kinda bittersweet. There's one stanza that always gets me cryin'.

JACKSON. *(Teasing her.)* And which "stanza"'s that?

JENNY. *(Slapping him playfully.)* At the end - "And the three men I admire most/ The Father, Son and the Holy Ghost/ They caught the last train for the coast/ The Day the music died."

JACKSON. The "stanza" that always gets me is "I was a lonely teenage broncin' buck/ With a pink carnation and a pickup truck/ But I knew I was out of luck/ The Day the music died." But my favorite line *(Begins singing.)* - "Them good old boys were drinkin' whiskey and rye..."

JACKSON AND JENNY. *(Singing.)* "...Singin' this'll be the day that I die/ This'll be the day that I die."

(JENNY breaks into laughter and JACKSON holds the last deep note, sounding awful.)

JACKSON. You ever heard the line he's gotta voice for radio? Well, I think I gotta voice for the shower. Or alone in my truck with all the windows rolled up. *(Pause.)* I like to listen to this song before games though.

JENNY. There's somethin' soothin' about it. My mamma used to sing it to me. *(They sit for a little, listening, swaying to the song.)* You ready for Friday night? *(Pause.)* Hmm, you probably get that question a lot.

JACKSON. I don't mind it. I'm always ready for Friday night. I wish I could live on that damn old football field.

JENNY. I never really understood why everyone in this town is so damn concerned with winnin'.

JACKSON. It's all they got. It's all I've got.

JENNY. I mean you're gonna win or you're gonna lose, but the sun's always gonna come up, birds are gonna chirp, smell of barbeque's gonna fill the air, sun's gonna set and before you know it it'll be Friday night again. We always set back into the same old routine. It wouldn't be the end of the world.

JACKSON. You've got a different mind set than almost everyone in this town. It's all they have to look forward to.

JENNY. *(Pause.)* You ever get butterflies?

JACKSON. Course. Right in here. It's the best kind of butterflies, though.

JENNY.   That's how I feel when I dream of traveling the world, seein' things, gettin' out, ya know?

JACKSON. I never dreamed of leavin'.

JENNY. Really? *(Gestures inside.)* Even with all that goin' on?

JACKSON.   They'd be fightin' if we were in California, or New York City, or China. It don't matter.

JENNY. We've been neighbors for a long while now, huh?

JACKSON. Guess so, 'bout three years since we moved next door. I kinda feel like I'm neighbors with everyone in this tiny town, though.

JENNY. Sometimes I feel like I'm trapped in a giant snow globe or somethin', and I'm just waiting for somebody to break the damn glass. Everyone knows everything about each other here. I'm ready to be someone new.

JACKSON. I don't think I know everythin' 'bout you at all, Jenny Slater.

JENNY.   There is a lot to learn...I'm an interestin'

gal. *(Cracks a smile.)*

JACKSON. *(Smiles. After a while.)* Thanks.

JENNY. For what?

JACKSON. Just for bein' here, I guess. It's pretty rare for people to stick around with me. I feel like we've sat on this old porch step together a lot in the past year, even if all we do is sit and listen to the screamin' inside, I'm glad to have someone around to listen with.

JENNY. Well, that *(Gestures inside where the screaming is escalating.)* is something I understand.

JACKSON. Really? I didn't have Mr. Slater pegged for the fightin' and yellin' type.

JENNY. He's not. That's exactly the problem...It sounds weird, but sometimes I just wish my parents would fight like that.

(The screaming escalates; a woman's voice says "Fuck you Jimmy!" loudly with a harsh southern twang.)

JACKSON. Like that? Really?!

JENNY. It'd be better than the whisper wars, the suffocating tension, fake smiles and deafening silence at the dinner table.

JACKSON. Well, you're welcome to my dinner table anytime. Actually, it's not quite a table. It usually consists of hot pockets and Easy Mac on my bedroom floor while I listen to some more of that. *(Nods his head towards the screaming.)*

JENNY. I don't know if I could resist an offer for free Easy Mac made by the town's one and only Jackson Bailey.

JACKSON. Kinda surprisin' 'bout your folks.

JENNY. Yeah, I don't think they're gonna split up or anything cause my mamma's been real sick for a while now. I think that's what stops them from that kinda fightin'. But sometimes I wish they'd split up.

Do I sound awful for sayin' so?

JACKSON. Nah, I used to think it'd be easier if my parents were far apart. To be honest, I don't really give a damn 'bout them anymore though.

JENNY. I wish I could do that.

JACKSON. What?

JENNY. Not give a damn.

JACKSON. Don't wish that. You've got too many good dreams and too much potential to not give a damn. Trust me, you'd think it's a carefree life, but it gets messy real quick. You stop carin' about anything and everythin' that ever mattered to you. Suddenly, you don't know how to get what you want anymore.

JENNY. But it'd be so much easier if I wasn't always tangled up in everyone else's mess.

JACKSON. I get that. But sometimes if you stop carin' 'bout everyone else, you suddenly stop carin' 'bout yourself, too, and you lose everything that's important to ya.

JENNY. You haven't lost everything.

JACKSON. *(After a while.)* Your folks expectin' you for dinner?

JENNY. They can do without me for a little longer.

JACKSON. I know Mr. Slater and your older brother, Sam, from football, but I don't know your mamma all too well, I always just say "Hey, Mrs. Slater" in passin'.

JENNY. She's pretty, even though sometimes she's real sad for many days at a time. But when she smiles...you'd just love her.

JACKSON. *(Looks at her, bittersweet, softer than usual.)* I bet I would.

JENNY. How bout your folks? What are they always worked up 'bout in there?

JACKSON.   Honestly I've lost track. It's always either about how we don't have enough money or about my dad abandonin' us again or about how much of a screw up I am. I'm over it all, but you know my brother, Quinn, he's only ten.

JENNY. Yeah, I'm the littlest one in my house, too. My older brother and sister were both kinda like you, tryin' to protect me and all.

JACKSON.   Yeah, I just wish he could stay ten forever, ya know? I wish I could put a ten year old force field around him where all he ever knew and cared about were Mr. Good Bars and catchin' toads from the pond and ridin' his bike. I try to stay like a ten year old. Those were the times. That's the last time I can remember havin' a real dream.

JENNY. You don't have any dreams now?! Don't you ever just wanna get out of here, Jackson?

JACKSON. I don't know. It sounds excitin' when you talk about it, but where would you go?

JENNY. I want to see every state in the U.S. The farthest I've been is 'bout 300 miles south to Austin. I wanna see the east and the west. I wanna see the beaches and the mountains. Dip my toes in the ocean. Meet new people, do new things.

It's probably not even what they mean in the song, but I wanna be Miss American Pie. I wanna see everything, go everywhere.

JACKSON. Wow, you dream big, Jenny Slater.

JENNY. Don't you want change? Opportunities? Possibility? I want to pack my bags and buy a plane ticket to anywhere and everywhere. I want to wake up to the smell of fresh coffee and the sound of the subway movin' through the city. I want to buy pretty dresses and wear them barefoot in the summer. I want to go to sleep in a town that's not still buzzed off the win from Friday night on Tuesday. I want a fresh opportunity each and every mornin'. I want to be on my own without the burden of everyone around me. I want to feel important in a place full of important people. Kinda like you.

JACKSON.   I'm not important, but I have lived some of my dreams. Mine were never that big, though. Football, a best friend, a pretty girl. That's all a man could dream for.

JENNY.   Dreams are important. It's what keeps us reachin', graspin'...

JACKSON.   My dreams are different from yours. Smaller.

JENNY.   There aint no such thing as a little dream.

JACKSON.   This little slice of American Pie is my dream.

(Screaming escalates from inside and a door slams. JENNY looks over at JACKSON who looks down, an ashamed look crossing over his face.)

JENNY.   You seem like a dreamer to me. I can see it deep down there. It's that look in your eyes. Only a fellow dreamer can recognize it...

JACKSON.   That means a lot comin' from you.

JENNY.   The sky looks real pretty tonight.

JACKSON.   Funny thing is it's the same sky out there in Georgia, California, New York, all those big, bright places you wanna see...but there's only one Texas.

JENNY.   *(Looks over to the suitcase.)* What's that for?

JACKSON.   My dad always packs his things and leaves 'em outside when they get into it like this, it's almost like a threat. Usually he ends up leavin' for a few weeks at a time. *(After a while, looks at JENNY).* Are you gonna leave, Jenny Slater?

JENNY. Not quite yet, Mr. Bailey. I think I'm gonna stick around here for a while longer...There is only one Texas.

(They smile at each other genuinely and innocently as JACKSON grabs the Walkman and presses play. The chorus of American Pie - Don McLean begins aloud as the lights fade.)

Harry the Hippo
By Megan Rivkin

Megan Rivkin

Megan Rivkin's short plays *Harry The Hippo* (LACPF, Skokie Theatre), *Camp Rivercreek* (Bergen County Academies), *Sexual Relations* (Manhattan Repertory Theatre), and *The Little Things* (Tufts University) have made it to the stage in recent years. She is a student at Tufts University and currently serves as Co-Artistic Director for the Bare Bodkin Theatre Company, a group dedicated to new and experimental works. She is writing an untitled full-length play and collaborating on a musical.
Visit her at: meganrivkin.com.

Harry the Hippo premiered in the Stevenson High School One-Act Festival in the spring of 2016. It was directed by Megan Rivkin. The stage manager was Andrew Hirsch. The cast was as follows:

Dave...Quinn Cunningham
Jeffrey....................................Andrew Projanksy
Laura..Kate Liebl

Harry the Hippo was part of the Skokie Short Play Theatre Festival in August, 2016. It was directed by Megan Rivkin. The cast was as follows:

Dave...Vlad Berez
Jeffrey......................................Scott Weinberg
Laura..Kate Liebl

Harry the Hippo received its west coast premiere in May 2018 as part of the Los Angeles Collegiate Playwrights Festival and was produced by Punk Monkey Productions at The Lounge Theatre 2 in Hollywood, CA. It was directed by Dan Fishbach. The lighting design was by Michael Massey. The board operator and stage manager was Jany Stehman. The cast was as follows:

Dave...Vince DonVito
Michael Taylor Gray
Jeffrey..Nick DiCola
Laura...Mary Carrig
Jessica Abrams

CHARACTERS:

>**DAVE:** Early 30's, Children's Book Writer
>**JEFFREY:** Early 30's, Children's Book Writer
>**LAURA:** Early 30's, Publishing Consultant

>*PLACE*
>*Office*

>*Lights up on a conference room, with a large table center. DAVE and JEFFREY sit at the table, a notepad and pens in front of each of them. Next to them is a white board with a colored-in cartoon hippo drawn on it.*

DAVE. *(Flipping through their manuscript of "Harry The Hippo".)* Honestly, I'm a little nervous to share this after our last set of edits.

JEFFREY. You know it's great. We've been working on making it more detailed for months. I think it's the best it's going to get.

DAVE. Yeah, you're probably right. We've just never presented to a consultant before.

JEFFREY. It's her job to give us some constructive criticism. Don't be nervous.

DAVE. Okay. Okay. You're right.

JEFFREY. *(Motions to the drawing of Harry on the whiteboard.)* And we're so prepared. We even have a draft from the illustrator.

(LAURA enters, carrying three coffee cups in a travel crate. She sets them down on the table.)

LAURA. Alright, let's get started, shall we? *(Pulls a binder out of her briefcase.)* Nice to meet you two. I'm Laura.

DAVE. *(Nervously.)* Dave.

JFFREY. *(Eager.)* Jeffrey.

LAURA. *(With disdain.)* Oh, such...masculine names. *(DAVE and JEFFREY share a look.)* Well, anyway, from what corporate tells me, you two are the best in the business. They just wanted me to come in and consult; to make sure what you've written will sell.

DAVE. *(Smiles.)* Well, "Harry The Hippo" is our most promising yet.

LAURA. If it's anything like "Sammy The Salamander", I'm excited to read it.

JEFFREY. *(Nostalgically.)* I love that one.

LAURA. Jeffrey, why don't you start by reading it aloud? It's important to get a sense of how the book will sound when parents are reading it to their kids.

JEFFREY. *(Clears his throat.)* Harry was a young hippo. Every day he-

LAURA. I'm sorry; I'm going to have to stop you right there.

JEFFREY. What?

LAURA. I don't want to be knit-picky, but in today's world, we can't really assign a gender to our characters, especially if they're young.

DAVE. *(Laughs.)* I'm sorry, what?

LAURA. *(Diplomatic.)* Gender is a very restrictive social construct. Children who identify with the opposite gender of Harry, or no gender at all, will feel marginalized.

JEFFREY. I...wouldn't have known that.

LAURA. That's why I'm here. Continue.

JEFFREY. Every day, he- I mean Harry- was woken up by his mommy and daddy.

LAURA. Oh no, that one's going to have to go.

DAVE. Why?

LAURA. The gay community will just have a fit.

DAVE. Isn't that...a bit dramatic?

LAURA.   That's   actually   a   very   offensive stereotype.

DAVE. I didn't mean- I would...say that about anyone. That's a silly reaction.

LAURA. *(Giving him a death stare, standing.)* The self-identifying gays in this country have been treated as second-class citizens for centuries. You're really going to continue the cycle of under-representing them?

JEFFREY. Well not anymore…

DAVE. So we should give Harry a pair of gay dads?

LAURA. Well, of course. And a pair of moms, too. I think that goes without saying.

(JEFFEREY and DAVE look at each other.)

JEFFREY. I'm not sure it does.

LAURA. *(Scolding.)* And don't call his pair of moms a pair of "gay moms." Just because two women are together, does not mean you can assume they are homosexuals.

JEFFREY. What?

LAURA.   21st   century   relationships   are complicated. We need to represent the modern, diverse family structure. Alright, Jeffrey, please continue.

JEFFREY. Every day, Harry's mom- I mean "moms" would give him a bath.

LAURA. Oh, right, having the women doing the cleaning.

JEFFREY. Uh, um, Harry's parents-es (not sure how to word the two sets of parents) would give him a bath. They made sure to scrub all over his grey skin.

LAURA.   *(Stands up, frustrated.)* Really? Bringing race into a book for impressionable children?

DAVE. You've got to be kidding me.

LAURA. *(Motioning to the whiteboard and walking over.)* May I?

JEFFREY. Um, sure. That's why we have a whiteboard-

LAURA. *(Whips back around.)* You mean "multiracial" board, not white board.

DAVE. Um...

(LAURA walks over to the white board and erases the color from the drawing of Harry.)

LAURA. You don't want children thinking that skin color is important.

DAVE. *(Quietly, to JEFFREY.)* Okay, now he just looks like "Airy" the Hippo.

JEFFREY. *(To LAURA.)* So, do we just cut that part?

LAURA. *(Trying to hold it together.)* Absolutely not. We don't want to teach these children to be colorblind. That's ignorant.

DAVE. Okay...Then what?

LAURA. Well, you have a few options here. Harry can be a rainbow, he can change colors for each day of the week, he can be transparent so every color shows through him. You just want to make sure people of all races can relate to him.

JEFFREY. I- I don't even know how to react to that.

LAURA. Thank goodness I'm here to get this sorted out before you went on to publish this. Jeffrey, go on.

JEFFREY. After his bath, Harry sat down to eat a bowl of cereal.

LAURA. *(As if this should go without saying.)* You need to be tolerant of the gluten intolerant.

DAVE. He eats some quinoa?

LAURA. Really, we shouldn't bring food into this at all. *(Trying to appeal to any sort of empathy left in* *them, though she's pretty sure there isn't any.)* Think about how the anorexic children reading this book will feel. Cut that part.

JEFFREY. Okay. *(Bracing himself.)* ...And then Harry goes outside to play some soccer.

LAURA. *(Shaking her head, as if this conversation is causing her physical pain.)* Extremely offensive to those with physical handicaps.

DAVE. He reads a book?

LAURA. No! People can read into that as a reference to him reading the Bible!

DAVE. What people?

LAURA. We need to be careful with our micro-aggressions and cultural appropriation.

JEFFREY. Those are just words. Now you're just saying words.

DAVE. My mind hurts.

LAURA. *(Yelling.)* You know whose minds also hurt? Kids with dyslexia who aren't even going to be able to read this book with all the large words you've used! Jeffrey, continue.

JEFFREY. *(Terrified.)* After a fun...activity- *(He looks to LAURA for approval. She nods.)* Harry goes inside to do his math homework.

DAVE. *(Sarcastically.)* Make sure to mention that it's common core.

LAURA. *(Standing angrily.)* Dave, you think because you're a man, you can do my job better than me?

JEFFREY. Just don't say anything.

LAURA. *(Impatient.)* Alright, last page, finish up.

JEFFREY. And then Harry crawls into bed, snuggles up with his blankie, and goes to sleep.

LAURA. Ohh, you've just made the assumption that everyone reading this book will be in a socioeconomic position that they can afford a bed. Welcome to twenty first century America, gentleman. Poverty surrounds us. Take off your white privilege blindfold and look around!

JEFFREY. *(Frustrated.)* Harry falls asleep. The end.

(LAURA paces, collecting herself. DAVE and JEFFREY wait nervously for her to say something. She looks up when she has cooled off.)

LAURA. Good, good. With the edits I think it's going to be a smash. Well, I really have to get going now. My son- I mean, child, Leaf, has an appointment with its aromatherapy acupuncturist. Thanks for meeting with me, gentleme- gentlepeople. Best of luck.

(LAURA exits.)

DAVE. I told you our last set of edits was a bust.

JEFFREY. I don't think that was really her problem with it.

DAVE. *(Looking at his watch.)* Oh, wow, sweetie, it's late. We've got to go pick up Basil from kindergarten.

JEFFREY. Oh, you're right.

(They pack up and stand up.)

DAVE. Okay, but it's not just me, right? She was really, really weird?

JEFFREY. Dave, please don't say such blatantly sexist things.

(They exit, hand in hand. Maybe JEFFREY kisses DAVE on the cheek.)

BLACKOUT.

Ghost Girl

By Covi Loveridge Brannan

Covi Loveridge Brannan

Covi Loveridge Brannan is an actress, playwright, and stage manager based in New York City. She began playwriting in high school where she participated as both an actor and writer in the annual Harvard Westlake Playwrights Festival. Her plays *Ghost Girl* (2014) and *In Passing* (2015, co-written by Sydney Concoff) were selected and produced by the festival. She later collaborated with Naked Angels and The New School to produce the debut production of her play *in the sea*. In May 2018, an excerpt from her full-length play *Force et Confiance*, about the legacies of 20th Century theatre giants Eva Le Gallienne and Eleonora Duse, was presented as part of The New York Public Library Shelf Life Project at the Lincoln Center Bruno Walter Auditorium. Additional works include *BIKE SHOP*, *Recipe for a Witch Hunt*, *The Man in the Window*, *The Virgin Mary Had Menstrual Cramps* and *Count Me*. Covi is currently pursuing her BFA (Dramatic Arts) and MA (Arts Management & Entrepreneurship) at The New School College of Performing Arts. www.coviloveridgebrannan.com.

Ghost Girl was part of the Harvard Westlake Playwrights Festival, April 25-27, 2014 in North Hollywood, CA. It was produced by Christopher Michael Moore and directed by Michelle Spears. The technical director was Andrew Villaverde. The cast was as follows:

Girl...Emma Pasarow
Boy...Quinn Luscinski

Ghost Girl was produced by Punk Monkey Productions at The Lounge Theatre in Hollywood, CA in May 2018. It was directed by James Elden. The lighting design was by Michael Massey. The board operator and stage manager was Jany Stehman. The cast was as follows:

Girl...Coco Lloyd
Boy...…...Nikolai Berk

FOR JUSTIN

CHARACTERS:

> **BOY:** Aged 17. He wears jeans, a white t-shirt, an open button-down shirt, slightly disheveled. He is a sweet, charismatic guy. He was happy. But then, he lost her. He blamed himself.
>
> **GIRL:** Aged 16 when lost. She wears a white dress, her hair is down, barefoot. In life, she was a quiet beauty with a clear laugh. She had a secret from her past. She blamed herself.
>
> *TIME: Any time from 1966 to present-day. It is early autumn.*
>
> *Setting: A graveyard. Just before dawn.*
> *A BOY and a GIRL.*
>
> *At rise: She sits on a headstone. He paces in front of her. The GIRL is a ghost. She looks perfect, polished, like a porcelain doll. The BOY has a flashlight, which is used throughout to light the scene. His backpack sits next to the GIRL. He shines his flashlight in her face. She's unphased.*

BOY. Wow. I, I can't--
GIRL. --believe it?
BOY. No. I can't...So, it's really--
GIRL. Yes.
BOY. And you're really--
GIRL. Right now.
BOY. With me?
GIRL. Yes.
(He kneels next to her.)

BOY. No, you can't be here.

GIRL. I am.

(He puts his hand up to her cheek. For reasons unexplainable, He is forced to stop short of touching her skin. The BOY looks to the GIRL for help. She shakes her head. The BOY lets his hand fall into his lap.)

BOY. I can't touch you.

GIRL. I'm dead.

BOY. So, that means you have to--

GIRL. Not for a little while.

BOY. Right. Okay...So, when you died, did it hurt?

GIRL. *(Smiles.)* No.

BOY. Then it was over-- quickly?

GIRL. Yes.

BOY. You felt nothing?

GIRL. Not a thing.

BOY. And then you were, just, gone?

GIRL. Not gone. Home.

BOY. So that means you want to go back.

GIRL. Not for a little while.

(He sits, playing with a piece of grass. She gets up.)

GIRL. Stand up.

BOY. What?

(Her smile stops him. With some difficulty, he stands. He watches her walk, effortlessly. Almost above the ground. She stands behind him.)

GIRL. Close your eyes.

BOY. But--

GIRL. Please?

(He closes his eyes.)

GIRL. It feels like a dream. A dream whose time is forever. First, it's like falling. Up. You can't find the bottom. But then, it's like flying through water. You feel it on the tips of your fingers and the droplets on your eyelashes. Soon, it's like dancing on wind. The hairs on your arms prick up and your nose turns pink. You flip in the air, and your heart comes out and flutters like a sparrow against your chest. It is new again. It's clean. And you are so happy. Too happy to cry. And someone reaches out...and holds your hand.

(*Beat.*)

(*He opens his eyes. She is looking into his. Somehow they are facing each other. Both their hands are in front of them. Their fingertips aligned. Like touching--if only they could.*)

(*Pause.*)

BOY. We can't touch.

GIRL. No. But this is real.

BOY. My dream. You came and told me. To come.

GIRL. I did.

(*Suddenly, the GIRL casts her eyes down. She gets up and walks away from the BOY.*)

GIRL. I had to.

BOY. Why?

GIRL. I had to make it stop.

BOY. Make what stop?

GIRL. No matter how hard I tried, it just wouldn't go away. I couldn't stop feeling it.

BOY. Feeling what?

(*He shines the flashlight into her eyes.*)

BOY. (*Gently.*) What were you feeling?

GIRL. Guilt.

(*Beat.*)

BOY. But, you have nothing to--

GIRL. Yours...It won't let me go.

(*The BOY drops the flashlight to his side.*)

GIRL.   When it first happened, I was waiting in perfect nothing. I could see it. The nothing. I could smell it. I could feel it-- But then there was this warmth. I felt warm. Like the sun was right there. That it was streaming through all of me. But it wasn't the sun. It was bigger than the sun! Bigger and more wonderful, because it could wrap itself around all of the nothing, fill it's every pore and make it warm! ...I was there, being filled with the warm, waiting in the beauty of the nothing-- the nothing except for the warm-- and then I felt it. A something. A cold something and a something too terrible to want to figure out what it was-- But I didn't need to figure it out because I knew. I had known that something for a long time and it hurt too bad not to know what it was...guilt...I could feel it. Right in my stomach.--But how could that be? I thought I had lost that feeling along with all the others and everything else. I thought I watched it fall sideways into the oblivion. It couldn't be the same feeling, but it was. I tried so hard to make it go away, but I couldn't. But, then, I realized. The most terrible thing. It all made sense--

BOY. What made sense?

GIRL. I couldn't make it go away because it wasn't mine. It wasn't my feeling.

BOY. It was mine.

GIRL. Yours.

BOY. *(Angry.)* How do you know?

GIRL. I could feel it.

BOY. HOW?

GIRL. *(Laughs.)* I don't know.

BOY. But you're dead!

GIRL. It doesn't matter.

BOY. Of course it matters! You're not supposed to feel anymore. Isn't that the whole point of it all? That it all stops? You stop feeling. The nothingness and that. Everything stops.

GIRL. Look, I don't know how and I don't know why, but I could feel it. More than I could feel anything. It was all I could feel. All that was there to feel, and I couldn't stop it because it wasn't mine. It wasn't my feeling. It wasn't mine to stop! It was out of my control. But it hurt and it tore and I didn't think I could take it much longer, but then I thought that if I could see you, and I could make you stop feeling it, then I could stop feeling it and then we could both stop.

BOY. Stop what?

GIRL. Feeling.

(Beat.)

(The BOY stands there not knowing what to say. He is flustered. She waits, expectantly. He reaches for his backpack and fumbles with the zipper.)

BOY. I brought food.

GIRL. I don't eat.

BOY. Right. Why would you?

(A soft wind rustles through the trees.)

(The BOY shines the flashlight at the trees.)

BOY. Did you have tell me to come here?

GIRL. I've never done this before!

BOY. Fine. Well, it's creepy.

GIRL. I have a time frame.

BOY. Something could pop out from behind, and get me, like--

(He flashes the light in all directions. The light rests on her.)

GIRL. A ghost?

(He opens his mouth to speak. Clears his throat. She starts laughing.)

GIRL.   Honestly, love. I'm sorry. It seemed appropriate.

(He stops and smiles. Listens to her laugh. He sits down

across from her. He takes a book out of his backpack. She is about to speak.)

BOY. I brought Shakespeare.

(She stops.)

BOY. He was your favorite.

GIRL. *(Smiles.)* He was. Which one?

(He leans back on his elbow and holds the play up precariously with one hand.)

BOY. Ah, "Be innocent of that knowledge, dearest chuck."

(She beams.)

GIRL. MacBeth!

(He shines the flashlight up into his own face.)

BOY. (Ominously.) MacBeth!

(He holds the book out to her. She forgets, eagerly reaches for it. Tries to grab it. Her hand stops short. She remembers, then draws her hand back.)

GIRL. Good choice.

(He watches her.)

BOY. I could read to you.

GIRL. We don't have that much time. That's not why we're here.

(He covers his face.)

GIRL. Tell me. I know you're scared. It's okay. Me, too. I won't tell anyone. Please. I promise.

(Another wind brushes past the trees. The BOY puts down the play and fumbles for the flashlight. The flashlight falls and the light goes out. He tries to turn it back on. It's useless. He sets it down and takes the play in his hands. He runs his finger along the edges.)

BOY. I could have stopped it. That night.

GIRL. What?

BOY. All you had to do was tell me--

GIRL. --Is that what this is about?

BOY. That you weren't ready.

GIRL. It wouldn't have mattered.

BOY. Why not? I would've waited until you were ready.

GIRL. The day never would have come.

BOY. I wouldn't have cared how long. I --

GIRL. I would never have been ready.

BOY. How can you know that?

GIRL. It wasn't you. "Canst thou not minister to a mind diseased. Pluck from the memory a rooted sorrow"

BOY. A rooted sorrow?

GIRL. It's me. My mind. It has nothing do with you--us.

BOY. Us.

(He throws the play on the ground and buries his head in his knees. He is crying.)

(She looks at him.)

GIRL. It's not your fault.

BOY. Oh, hell!

GIRL. I'm serious. It's really not. I don't know why you'd think that it was.

(He laughs.)

BOY. HA! Oh, GOD. Don't say that to me.

GIRL. What do you mean?

BOY. You can't tell me what I can think! You don't know.

GIRL. Don't know what?

BOY. Anything!

GIRL. I don't understand.

BOY. Exactly! How could you? You didn't give me a chance? *(Pause.)* How could you do that? To me. Leave me like that.

GIRL. I didn't want--

BOY. I know that now.

GIRL. That's not what I meant.

BOY. I didn't know how upset you--And then you just left? You left me sitting in the car. I looked out the window, and, I could just barely see you in the dark. Running home. It was past two. You could barely see a thing--pitch black. I was so mad. I just sat there for hours until I could think enough to go home...It's not like I was trying to offend you. I know I should've asked, but/ would you have answered?

GIRL. Would you have listened?

BOY. *(Beat.)* I woke up and I was in my jeans. I couldn't remember how I got inside. I had a key, but it was probably a window. I came downstairs, in my jeans, put a Strawberry Pop-tart in the toaster, turned around and everyone was up. Staring at me. I looked back, but they didn't say anything. So I went and got my Pop-tart and sat at the table without a plate. My mom said nothing. She looked so tired...They didn't know how to say it. They didn't know how to "break the news". But they finally did. They said you had been hit. You were gone. And that they were sorry...And do you know what I did? I sat there eating that freaking Strawberry Pop-tart. It scared my own mother. She tried to put her hand on my shoulder and I pushed her. Then she just stared at me. I stood up, and I couldn't say anything. I knew she was just trying to help, but I didn't want her. I wanted-- So, I ran. I hated myself. For hurting her. For hurting you. I hated you. I hated you so much for doing this to me. I wanted you to come back just so I could grab you and kill you myself...And then I stopped running. Because I got to the spot. Where we had parked the night before. And I thought I saw you. Saw you, there, running home through the night. But then you were gone. So I sat there in the street. In my jeans. And cried. Because you weren't running home. You were running away. From me.

(Pause.)

GIRL. I don't know what to do.

BOY. You can't do anything!

GIRL. But I can't go like this!

BOY. You know what? That's a lie. Explain. Go on! Tell me. Why? Why did you leave?

(She sits there in silence and shock. He waits expectantly.)

(Beat.)

(Light begins to peak through on the horizon. A bird starts chirping. She looks out and watches the Sun.)

GIRL. It will be morning soon.

BOY. Are you joking? I just spilled my heart out and this is what you start telling me? Why, why did you leave?

GIRL. I was tired.

BOY. Tired?

GIRL. No, I mean. I can't go back without— *(She looks up.)* The Sun...I felt like the Sun.

BOY. Please, don't start with your weird metaphor thing.

GIRL. Just listen...I felt like the Sun. She shines each day, whether she wants to or not. It is her duty. She comes back each day to hide the stars. The memories. Some rage, some burn. You were my brightest star. Raging, caressing, consuming. Christmas. You were brightest, but not the only one. Some envelop, others burn. Burn and pierce and singe.

(As they talk, the Sun rises in the sky.)

GIRL. Not the same, but connected, constellations. Invisible lines. One leads to the other. So, in order to block out the one, the Sun is forced to cover them all. The Sun spreads over them. She spreads herself thin. She reaches, but never far enough.

BOY.   Okay, but when the Sun shines, you can't really see them anymore, the stars. The memories, the ones that burn. So they don't really matter.

GIRL.   When She shines her brightest they fade, but it's exhausting. The burning ones are always there. Her light always dims. Everlasting.

(The Birds begin chirping. They get louder and louder.)

BOY.   So, you were tired of what? Of living?

GIRL.   Covering a sky of stars is a lot of work. The Sun's work is constant. Each morning She rises and has to last all day.

(Pause.)

GIRL.   She exhausts herself, reaching and spreading and shining.

(The Birds stop chirping. It is morning.)

GIRL.   So, when night finally comes, She is relieved. The stars taunt and tease and pull, and remind her of her sin, but She doesn't have to shine anymore. It's night. Quiet. The secret, the stain She's tried to hide is still there, but when night comes, she doesn't have to cover and shine for anyone. She doesn't have to pretend.

(Beat.)

BOY.   What sin?

GIRL.   It was her duty. To stretch and maintain and cover. But She wanted to erase--

BOY.   Erase what? Her sin?

GIRL.   It was too hard. Nothing worked.

(A long silence.)

GIRL.   She was so young. She tried to run, but it was too late. The darkness took her for his own. And She was trapped. She let him inside. And now

she was his. Forever.
(Beat.)
BOY. You were...
(She looks away. Nods "yes".)
BOY. And when I touched you, you--
GIRL. Felt.
BOY. Him?
GIRL. So I ran.
BOY. Out of the car.
GIRL. Into the Night. The quiet.
BOY. Ran away.
GIRL. Yes. But not from you. From me.
(Beat.)
BOY. It wasn't...
(She shakes her head "no".)
GIRL. It had nothing to do with you.
(He exhales.)
BOY. I can breathe.
(The Girl is silent.)
BOY. The feeling in my stomach. The guilt. It's gone.
GIRL. *(Panicked.)* No, it isn't.
BOY. *(With relief.)* Everything is open.
GIRL. It's not. I, I can still feel it. My stomach. It's still there. Oh, no! No...
(She collapses to her knees. Holds her head between her knees.)
(Pause.)
BOY. I'm sorry.
GIRL. No, don't apologize. I'm so selfish. I came here to make you feel better and you do. And, I don't know why I feel the same, but that's not what's important. I'm happy that you feel better. That's why I came.
BOY. Listen to me! The man. The one--

GIRL. I don't want to talk about it.

BOY. No. Look at me.

GIRL. I can't, I--

BOY. He was sick. He did something terrible.

GIRL. *(Barely audible.)* I did it, too.

BOY. What? No. You were a little girl. You couldn't have stopped him...Lena.

(She looks up at him. Remembering.)

BOY. How old were you? Eight? Seven?

(She doesn't move.)

BOY. Even if you tried--

GIRL. --But he told me--

BOY. --You wouldn't have been able to do anything. He was a grown man. You were too young. It wasn't you. You were too young to be a Sun. Covering the sin. The duty, the responsibility wasn't yours.

GIRL. I know that.

BOY. Clearly you don't know that. No part of this is your fault. You think that by somehow you not being able to stop it or do anything that makes it your fault, but it doesn't. He lied to you.

GIRL. He was lying.

BOY. And his lies were not for you to cover up.

(Beat.)

(He waits. Searching her eyes. She glows. She starts to cry. It goes on. And he waits. The light of daybreak. The GIRL looks to the horizon. She inhales.)

GIRL. *(Exhaling.)* I can breathe.

(She looks at him.)

GIRL. I wish I would've told you.

BOY. It's okay.

(A sadness passes between them. He goes to hold her-- remembers. The BOY steps forward. He stands with his arms outstretched, throws his head back. He starts

singing "Wouldn't It Be Nice?" by The Beach Boys.)
BOY.   *(Sings, loudly.)* "Wouldn't it be nice if we were older? Then we wouldn't have to wait so long."
(She looks up.)
BOY. *(Cont'd. singing.)* "And wouldn't it be nice to live together. In the kind of world where we belong."
(She smiles. He bows, offers her his hand. She gets up and bows. He signals her to spin around. She laughs and does.)
BOY. *(Cont'd. singing.)* "You know it's gonna make it that much better. When we could say good night, and stay together! WOULDN'T IT BE NICE!"
(They fall down next to each other. Laughing.)
GIRL. *(Gently.)* I miss hugging you.
BOY. I miss you, too.
(Beat.)
(They look into the horizon. It is morning.)
BOY. Will you ever come back?
GIRL. I don't think I need to.
(She smiles.)
BOY. Right. So, now, it's okay. You can go.
GIRL. Where?
BOY. Home.
(The GIRL turns to face the horizon.)
(She waits. For a second, she doesn't know if she wants to go.)
(She turns and looks at the BOY. He is smiling. She smiles back and walks into the light.)
(She is gone.)
(We can now see the full extent of the graveyard. Headstones adorned with bouquets of flowers are revealed in the background.)
(The BOY gathers his things, puts the flashlight in his

backpack.)
(He picks up the book. He gets on his knees.)
(He lays down the book where she sat.)
(He kisses the tip of his fingers and presses his finger to the cover.)
(Beat.)
(The BOY stands reluctantly. He looks into the horizon.)
(He puts on his backpack and walks off into the graveyard. He is gone.)
(The stage fades to light.)

END OF PLAY.

Acknowledgements

Thank you to Christopher Michael Moore for extending an opportunity so many years ago that led to multiple productions and newfound passions as well as the completion of this book.

Help spread the word and support the Los Angeles Collegiate Playwrights Festival by following and "liking" us on the social media platforms below or visiting us at www.lacpfest.com. By doing so, you will be kept up to date on submission opportunities as well as performance dates and other announcements pertaining to the Los Angeles Collegiate Playwrights Festival.

🅵 fb.com/lacpfest

🐦 @lapfest

📷 @lacpfest